Recyclone Returns

or

*The 25th anniversary of a recycling superhero
and his battle against global warming*

Text and illustrations copyright 2013 by Lee P. Sauer
Printed in the United States
ISBN-13: 978-1493664759
ISBN-10: 1493644750

Summary: The 3-R's (recycling, reducing, reusing) need a superhero. Hello! It's The Recyclone, a muscle-bound goof with a big smile. Whenever he sees recyclables trapped in ordinary trash, Recyclone turns into a whirlwind of activity. His goal? To save the earth! The Recyclone comic strip ran from 1988 to 1992. On the 25th anniversary of the strip, creator Lee P. Sauer takes a look back at the times, the drawings, and the stage shows. All 133 Recyclone comic strips included. Does this mean the earth is saved? Stay tuned.

C&C Press
www.drawingsmiles.com
recyclone@yahoo.com

To my girls:

MacKenzie, Morgan and Avrie

What is this book about?

The Recyclone, superhero of the recycling movement.

Hi, there. Welcome to *Recyclone Returns*.

What, you may ask, is this book about?

A comic strip titled *The All New Adventures of The Recyclone* appeared weekly (well, almost weekly) from Nov. 26, 1988, to July 11, 1992, in the *Evening Star* newspaper of Auburn, IN. A bumbling musclehead dressed in tights played the title role.

Dubbed "superhero of the recycling movement," Recyclone simple-mindedly pursued a single goal—to save the earth. In his war against waste, he battled one garbage can at a time. Whenever encountering recyclables trapped in ordinary, household trash, Recyclone turned into a whirlwind of activity, rescued newspapers, bottles, and cans, and delivered them safely to the nearest recycling center.

Think it's campy? Melodramatic? Good. You've got the concept.

This book commemorates the 25th anniversary of The Recyclone comic strip. It contains all of the original cartoons, examples of other artwork in which Recyclone appeared, and a photo from the stage shows. (More on the stage shows later.) I have added notes on people, places and events of the time to put the material in context.

And who the heck am I? I am a former, mild-mannered newspaper reporter and the only person who can contact Recyclone directly. Recyclone depends on me to speak for him. But more on that later, too.

For now, enjoy the book . . .

Oh, and keep recycling!

Lee P. Sauer
October 16, 2013

Recyclone turns into a whirlwind of activity whenever he sees recyclable bottles, cans and newspapers trapped in ordinary, household trash.

"The Recyclone" or "Recyclone?"

Of course, the name, "Recyclone," comes from the words *recycling* and *cyclone*.

But you may notice indecision on whether the official name is "The Recyclone" or simply "Recyclone." In early strips, I insisted that our superhero be known as "The Recyclone." I had it in my head that the name represented a contraction of *"The Recycling One."*

But it was a lonely battle. Everyone else called him "Recyclone." I finally gave in.

The Beginning

I remember when Recyclone first came to me. As a newspaper reporter, I attended a meeting of a grassroots recycling group. The group asked if I could convince the paper to run a weekly (and free) tidbit of recycling news. Sure, I replied, not certain I could deliver on the promise.

At that time, I had been employed at the *Evening Star* of Auburn, IN, only a few weeks. No one—not members of the recycling group, fellow reporters, or the paper's leadership—knew I wanted to be a cartoonist. I had been looking for an opportunity to draw. This was it!

On dark streets during the walk back to the office, a bumbling, self-absorbed, absent-minded superhero visited me. I sketched the first strip that night.

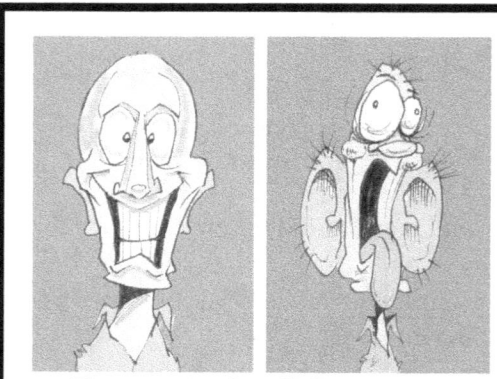

The narrator, Lee P. Sauer, as he appeared in 1988, and as he appears today.

Evening Star editor, David Kurtz, as he appeared in 1988, and as he appears today.

The following day, I presented the idea to the Star's editor, David Kurtz. He sniffed, shrugged and said, "Sure, we'll run it."

The first five cartoons appear on the following pages. Each strip is numbered. If notes apply to a particular cartoon, I will refer to it by number.

For example: The towns of Butler and Garrett get notice in strips #3 and #4. Both towns can be found near Auburn in northeast Indiana. Kaukauna, written on the postcard in #5, lies in Wisconsin's Fox Valley. It gained fame as my folks' hometown at the time.

#1, *Initial Introduction*, November 26, 1988

#2, *Arresting Idea*, December 3, 1988

#3, *Markle Noogie*, December 10, 1988

#4, *Wet Tie Treatment*, December 17, 1988

#5, *Christmas Postcard*, December 24, 1988

How to dig through trash and be cool

Re-reading these strips, I'm reminded of recycling's place in the world 25 years ago. Most folks considered recycling geeky, radical, the strange obsession of twig munchers. Comedians poked fun at people on the environmental fringe—people like Euell Gibbons, who starred in TV commercials for Grape Nuts cereal and famously asked, "Ever eat a pine tree?"

See Euell Gibbons *for yourself:* www.youtube.com/watch?v=_XJMIu18I8Y

Recycling took real effort. First, you sorted recyclables out of your trash. Then you drove to a recycling center to drop them off. Recycling centers were small, difficult to find and took only the basics: newspapers, glass bottles and aluminum cans. Often staffed by volunteers, each center remained open only certain days and limited hours. So a recycler needed to be self-motivated and well-informed.

I hoped Recyclone would make kids want to recycle. He might show that saving the earth could be simple, fun and rewarding. He might even make recycling cool!

Moonbeam

The second recurring character, known simply as Moonbeam, appeared for the first time in #9, *Moonbeam Fashion Tip*.

My sister, Jane, inspired Moonbeam's look. Karen Farlow, one of the grassroot recycling group organizers, inspired Moonbeam's radical approach to recycling. (See box)

Moonbeam

Recyclone and Moonbeam's relationship evolved over the run of the strip. At first Moonbeam played her role with a stoic, business-like attitude. Later, Moonbeam became leader of the team. She provided the practical, reasonable mind behind Breeze Brain's silly slapstick. Occasionally her frustration boiled over and she bossed Recyclone around.

In the final stage, Moonbeam played a lovesick teenager, longing for recognition from her boss. Why? I don't know. Every good story needs a little sexual tension, I guess.

Real-life superhero

Karen Farlow of Auburn, IN, played multiple roles in Recyclone's success.

Karen provided material for comic strips. She played Moonbeam in the early stage shows. (More on the stage shows later.) And she tirelessly promoted all aspects of recycling.

Karen Farlow

This book would not have been possible without Karen—literally. When the strip's run ended, Farlow handed me a vanilla file folder. It contained every Reyclone comic, neatly snipped out of the paper and placed in chronological order.

#7, *Can Crusher*, January 7, 1989

THE RECYCLONE — by LEE P.

RECYCLONE, HERE, TO TEACH YOU...

ANY TIME YOU RE-USE MATERIAL, YOU ARE RE-CYCLING

THE WORD "RECYCLE" COMES FROM THE GREEK GOD "RE-CYCLOMUS," WHO WON THE HEART OF THE FAIR LAND-FILLIA WITH A SLEEVELESS SWEATER HE SALVAGED FROM THE TRASH CAN OF VENUS.

TODAY, REUSING CLOTHES AS HAND-ME-DOWNS IS RECYCLING...

COLD STEW

COOL WHI

REUSING PLASTIC FOOD CONTAINERS TO STORE LEFTOVERS IS RECYCLING...

REUSING TIRES AS SWINGS IS RECYCLING!

RECYCLING ISN'T JUST COLLECTING NEWSPRINT, ALUMINUM AND GLASS. RECYCLING IS REUSING MATERIALS TO MAKE LESS TRASH!!

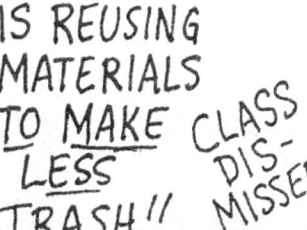

CLASS DIS-MISSED!

#9, *Moonbeam Fashion Tip,* **January 28, 1989**

THE RECYCLONE by LEE P.

RECYCLONE, HERE!

HAVE YOU BEEN SAVING NEWSPRINT TO RECYCLE?

WELL THEN, LOAD IT IN YOUR FAVORITE MODE OF LOCO-MOTION

LOCOMOTE TO THE MOOSE PARKING LOT IN AUBURN

MOOSE

MAIN STREET

TENTH STREET

LEEP

THEN UNLOAD IT AT BOY SCOUT TROOP 175's PAPER DRIVE

UNG!

OR, LET ONE OF THE SCOUTS UNLOAD IT FOR YOU!

PANT PANT

HEH-HEH! STRONG LITTLE NIPPER!

DO IT RIGHT NOW! TODAY! FEBRUARY 4TH! BEFORE 2 P.M.! OR YOU WON'T HAVE ANOTHER CHANCE UNTIL THE FIRST SATURDAY OF NEXT MONTH!

P.S. ALL PROCEEDS GO TO TROOP 175

The Bulk Trash Dragon

Bulk Trash Dragon

Recyclone's archenemy, The Bulk Trash Dragon, makes its first appearance in #18, *Sortin' Swoon*.

The mute beast suffers an insatiable appetite for trash. And, as he eats, he grows. The dragon plays a larger and more sinister role in *The Recyclone's Epic Adventure*, #40-57.

> **Shout out**
>
> Andrew Kurtz, a.k.a. "Boo," son of Evening Star Editor Dave Kurtz, receives a shout-out in #12. A frequent visitor to the newsroom, Boo hit for average in our office tape ball games and played second base. He also claimed to enjoy reading the comic strips.

The stage shows

Okay, *NOW* I'll tell about the stage shows.

Within weeks after the strip debuted, a school called to ask if Recyclone could visit and talk to students. Then a recycling center called. Then another school called. And another.

I talked to Recyclone about performing live, in front of an audience. He reluctantly agreed. (Actually, once he gets in front of a crowd, he's quite a ham.) Soon we were traveling across Indiana, Ohio and Michigan, teaching anyone who would listen about the 3-R's. (Recycle, Reduce, Reuse.)

Recyclone appeared onstage with Union Elementary School teacher Charles Cragen in this photo, which appeared in the Johnson County (Indiana) Daily Journal on Friday, November 14, 1997.

"We?"

Yes, we. I traveled with Recyclone. He needed someone to set up props, make arrangements, wrtie scripts. We worked as a team. You might say we became inseparable.

Sheryll Prentice, dressed as Moonbeam.

In early versions of the show, Moonbeam appeared onstage with Recyclone. At first, Karen Farlow (see page 8) served as Recyclone's assistant. Later, Sheryl Prentice, community news editor for the Evening Star, took on Moonbeam's duties.

Whenever Recyclone first appeared onstage, he greeted the audience with the catchphrase, "Hi, there. I'm The Recyclone!"

The stage shows outlived both the strip and my employment at the newspaper. I left the Star in 1995 to pursue freelance opportunities. The last Recyclone show took place in 2000.

THE RECYCLONE — by LEE P.

AUTHOR, HERE!

YOU AIN'T MY VALENTINE

(A BALLAD BY **THE RECYCLONE**)

I COULD LOVE YOU EVEN THOUGH
YOU DON'T TELL ME THE WHOLE TRUTH
I COULD LOVE YOU EVEN THOUGH
YOU HAVE A RATHER LARGE CABOOSE

I COULD LOVE YOU EVEN THOUGH
YOU DON'T TOE MY CREDIT LINE
I COULD LOVE YOU EVEN THOUGH
YOUR HYGIENE IS BOVINE

I COULD LOVE YOU EVEN THOUGH
YOU DON'T GARGLE WITH LAVORIS
I COULD LOVE YOU EVEN THOUGH
YOU SAT ON MY CAT MORRIS

ON THIS DAY OF LOVE, DEAR,
I COULD ASK YOU TO BE MINE
BUT SINCE YOU DON'T RECYCLE
YOU AIN'T _MY_ VALENTINE!!

LEE P

SAME TO YA, BREEZE BRAIN!

TAP TAP

#12, *T-Shirt Shill,* **February 18, 1989**

#14, *Naked Ambition*, March 6, 1989

THE RECYCLONE
by LEE P.

TODAY I'M TOO EXCITED TO SAY, "RECYCLONE HERE!"

BOING!

AUBURN MAY BE GETTING A PERMANENT RECYCLING DROP-OFF CENTER!!

- IT <u>COULD</u> BE SET UP IN THE <u>OLD</u> ELECTRIC BUILDING ON SOUTH WAYNE STREET
- IT <u>MAY</u> BE OPEN EVERY FRIDAY AND SATURDAY STARTING MAY 6TH.
- ALL THE COULDs AND MAYs AND HOW-TOs WILL BE DECIDED BY AUBURN CITY GOVERNMENT <u>SOON</u>!!

IF THE CENTER BECOMES REALITY, I'LL GROW HUGE AND POWERFUL!! NO GARBAGE WILL BE SAFE!!

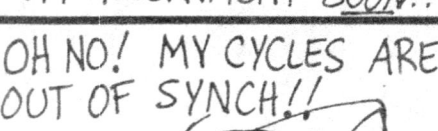

OH NO! MY CYCLES ARE OUT OF SYNCH!!

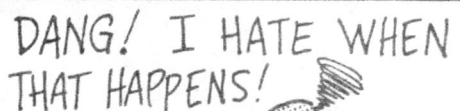

DANG! I HATE WHEN THAT HAPPENS!

#16, *Dose of Reality*, March 18, 1989

#17, *Clodhopper Crush*, March 27, 1989

#18, *Sortin' Swoon*, April 3, 1989

#19, *No License Required*, April 10, 1989

#20, *Damp Newsprint*, April 22, 1989

#21, *He'll Be Back,* **April 29, 1989**

THE RECYCLONE IS EXHAUSTED, WHAT WITH ALL THE APPEARANCES AT DEPARTMENT STORES AND SCHOOLS AND **AUBURN'S RECYCLING CENTER,** NOW OPEN AT THE JUNCTION OF WAYNE AND MAIN STREETS (FRIDAYS 10 A.M. TO 5 P.M. ; SATURDAYS 8 A.M. TO NOON)

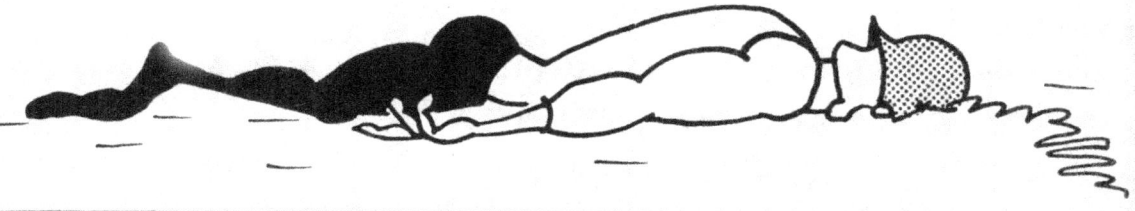

OUR SUPER HERO WILL, REGRETTABLY, BE BACK TO FULL STRENGTH NEXT WEEK.

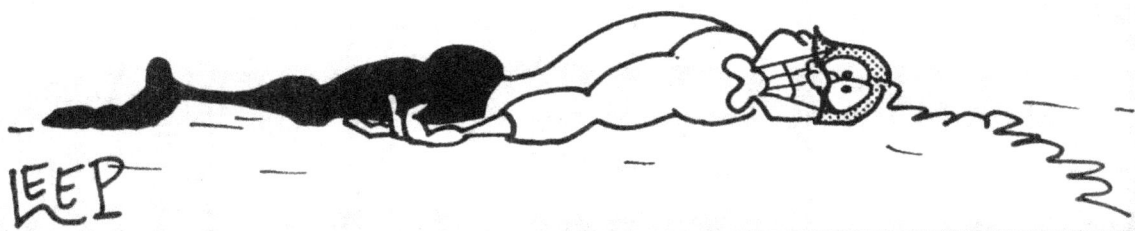

RECYCLONE, HERE! THE AUBURN RECYCLING CENTER'S GRAND OPENING WAS A GREATER SUCCESS THAN MOST PEOPLE REALIZE!

MOONBEAM! TOSS ME THE BUNDLE OF NEWSPAPERS WE COLLECTED!

ARE YOU SURE? IT'S QUITE A BUNDLE!

HEH HEH HEH! SILLY GIRL! I'M A SUPER HERO, REMEMBER?

WE PROVED THE CRITICS WRONG IN A *BIG* WAY! THEY SAID AUBURN RESIDENTS WOULDN'T RECYCLE. BUT WAIT TILL YOU SEE WHAT WE COLLECTED. MOONBEAM! WHERE ARE YOU?!

I'M READY. ARE *YOU* READY?

OF COURSE *I'M* READY!!

HEH HEH! SILLY GIRL!

COPYRIGHT LEE P. 1989

THE RECYCLONE   by LEE P.

SOME PEOPLE SEEM TO THINK THAT THE RECYCLING WORK IN DEKALB COUNTY IS ALL DONE!

ZZZ NNNNK KK

SOME PEOPLE THINK — NOW THAT AUBURN, BUTLER, GARRETT AND WATERLOO HAVE RECYCLING PROGRAMS — THAT NOW IS THE TIME TO REST!

Z NK K

LEEP

① BZZZZZZZZ..!!

②

SLAM!!   ③

THOSE PEOPLE ARE SADLY MISTAKEN!

MOI?

QUICK! BEFORE YOU RAISE THE IRE OF MOONBEAM, TAKE YOUR ALUMINUM, GLASS, NEWSPAPERS AND PLASTICS TO DEKALB COUNTY'S TWO PERMANENT RECYCLING CENTERS —

AUBURN: IN A STREET DEPT. BUILDING AT THE JUNCTION OF WAYNE AND MAIN STREETS 10 A.M.-5 P.M. FRIDAYS; 8 A.M. TO NOON SATS.

BUTLER: IN THE CITY BARN AT 100 W. DEPOT ST. OPEN 24 HOURS A DAY!!

* GARRETT AND WATERLOO R-DAYS WILL BE SCHEDULED AT FUTURE DATES!

#24, *Cure For Smelly Feet*, June 15, 1989

Recycling? Bah, humbug!

Despite Recyclone's generally warm welcome, resistance to recycling reared its head. Twenty five years ago, most folks believed trash reduction unnecessary. Some people saw recycling—even though it was voluntary at this point—as a restriction of their freedom.

Since Recyclone served as the face of recycling for our community, he received the complaints. And since I opened his mail, I read the complaints.

I would have bet that everyone could get behind a grassroots movement that didn't take much effort and would benefit generations to come. I would have lost the bet, as Recyclone does in #25.

Marketing mayhem

On Sept. 2, 1989, Recyclone marched in the Auburn-Cord-Duesenberg Festival Parade through downtown Auburn. I printed cartoon #27 on t-shirts and sold them to parade watchers.

Or, tried to.

Somewhere in my closet sits a box of unsold shirts.

Marketing for the movie *Batman* seemed out of control in the fall of 1989. Batman's likeness appeared everywhere. The marketing was so over-the-top, it became the butt of jokes. But Recyclone had no qualms about hitching the recycling movement to the movie's notoriety. (#29)

Cubs win? Really?

#31 proves how long ago Recyclone came onto the scene. The Chicago Cubs were good.

The baseball team made it into the playoffs in 1989 and clinched the National League East title with a 3-2 win over Montreal on September 26.

Harry Caray announced it with his patented, "Cubs win!"

Smell the fair in the air

Fresh, sugar-coated donuts. Italian sausage sandwiches with grilled onions and peppers. Oil-hot elephant ears. Sticky taffy apples. A mechanical clang and hiss. Bright, colored lights. Lowing cows. Neighing horses. A hint of hay riding on crisp, clean, fall air. Guys in sleeveless shirts and baseball caps; gals in jeans and cowboy hats.

That's the DeKalb County Fair. (#30)

My first visit to Auburn took place during the fair. I remember stepping over bundled snakes of electrical cords and pushing through crowds on my way to the newspaper office for an interview.

You could feel electricity in the air. The fair brought excitement—along with all kinds of livestock—to downtown Auburn.

#25, *Unconsciousableness*, June 21, 1989

#27, *Auto-Matic*, September 2, 1989

#29, *Batkid and Recyclone*, September 16, 1989

#30, *Beware of the Fair,* **September 23, 1989**

#31, *Cubs Win! Cubs Win!* October 7, 1989

#32, *For God and Country*, November 14, 1989

Willoughby, the non-talking horse

A horse named Willoughby makes his debut in #33, *The Culture of Trash*. Willoughby generally keeps his mouth shut. He's the strong, silent type, always willing to lend a hand . . . or hoof.

Willoughby

Numbers tell the story

Progress has been made since *Scary Stats #34* ran. Several websites put the current percentage of Americans who don't recycle at 23%. The website cited in the box below breaks the statistic down by age and region.

See **What Percent of Americans Recycle** *for yourself:*

www.environmentalleader.com/2007/08/28/25-of-americans-dont-recycle

Deadline dread

Giving Thanks (#36) reminds me of the constant pressure of producing Recyclone strips. Obviously my drawing skills weren't well developed, so each cartoon took time and effort. The strip could be compared to having a college term paper due each week. On the day before Thanksgiving in 1989, I wanted to be on the road to get to a family get-together. To save time, I made use of the newspaper's new copy machine. (Note that the first five panels are exactly the same.)

Not in my back yard

Twenty five years ago, environmentalists expressed concern that the United States would run out of landfill space. News agencies dissected the problem from every angle. Americans were producing more trash than ever. Plus, homeowners fought against the expansion of existing landfills and the building of new ones. These attitudes squeezed landfills from both sides. The acronym NIMBY summed up the problem. The letters stood for Not In My Back Yard.

Indiana environmentalists became particularly upset when they learned that landfills within our state accepted trash from the East Coast. *Hoosier Sell Out*, #39, refers to the problem.

And why were eastern states shipping their trash to the Midwest? They had run out of landfill space and their residents would not allow them to build more.

#33, *The Culture of Trash*, November 21, 1989

#34, *Scary Stats,* **November 4, 1989**

#35, *Shakespearean Solution*, November 11, 1989

#36, *Giving Thanks*, November 28, 1989

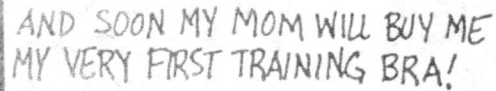

#37, *Christmas Wish,* **December 2, 1989**

#38, *Stressed for the Holidays,* **December 9, 1989**

An epic undertaking

For the first time in *The Recyclone's Epic Adventure* (#40-57), the comic strip attempts to tell an ongoing story over a number of weeks.

Several cultural signs of the times show up in this series. Indiana native Dan Quayle stumbles into national politics. Wal-Mart invades the Midwest, building gigantic stores in small towns and steamrolling locally-owned businesses. Stylish folks swoon over L.L. Bean products. Ickey Woods, a running back for the Cincinnati Bengals, dances his way to fame.

For the first time, it seems socially acceptable—even cool—to be spoiled, wealthy and shallow.

Recyclone swims against the current. He attempts to get folks to cooperate, to sacrifice, to pull toward a common goal.

In the climax of the Epic Adventure, Recyclone asks the whole world to join in "The Sortin' Shuffle." Our hero shows the audience motions that are done in time to the tune of *The Hokey-Pokey*. As recyclers dance, they sing: "Recycle, reduce and reuse trash, 'cause that's what it's all about!"

Will there be a happy ending? You be the judge.

#40, *Epic Adventure A*, January 6, 1990

#41, *Epic Adventure B*, January 13, 1990

#42, *Epic Adventure C*, January 20, 1990

#43, *Epic Adventure D*, January 27, 1990

CONTINUED FROM LAST WEEK...
RUN! RUN FOR YOUR VERY LIVES!!
THE BULK TRASH DRAGON IS AWAKE!!!

LAND FILL

THE LARGE, SMELLY MONSTER ATTRACTED PUBLIC ATTENTION.
OOOOO YUK!

A POLITICIAN ARRIVED.
STAND BACK, FOLKS! I'LL TAKE CARE OF THIS!

A POLICY WAS STATED.
LISTEN HERE, YOU OVERGROWN SLOP BUCKET, WE DON'T WANT YOU AROUND HERE, SO SCAT!!

COPYRIGHT LEEP. 1990

A RESPONSE WAS TENDERED.
BLAH!!

AN IMPASSE WAS REACHED.
DURN CRITTER YACKED ON ME!
GA-ROSS!!

TO BE CONTINUED....

#44, *Epic Adventure E,* February 3, 1990

#45, *Epic Adventure F*, February 17, 1990

#46, *Epic Adventure G*, March 3, 1990

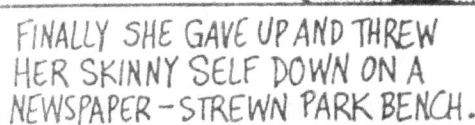

#47, *Epic Adventure H*, March 10, 1990

#49, *Epic Adventure J*, March 31, 1990

#50, *Epic Adventure K*, April 7, 1990

CONTINUED FROM LAST WEEK...
THE BULK TRASH DRAGON'S GREETING WAS DISGUSTING.

YUCK!

NO, "YAK."

THAT MIGHT HAVE DETERRED A LESSER SUPERHERO, BUT NOT THE RECYCLONE!

PREPARE TO BE SORTED, FOUL (AND MIGHT I ADD, SMELLY?) FIEND!

THE CLONE SORTED...

AND SORTED...

...AND SORTED!!

HOW AM I DOING? PANT PANT

LESSEE...

WELL, IF HE QUIT EATING, YOU'D BE DONE BY THE YEAR 2090!

THE PROBLEM IS, HE WON'T STOP EATING!

WELL, HE CAN'T EAT FASTER THAN I CAN SORT, CAN HE?

WANNA BET?!

N.J.

LEEP

CONTINUED...

#51, *Epic Adventure L*, April 14, 1990

#52, *Epic Adventure M,* **April 28, 1990**

by LEE P.

THE RECYCLONE MAKES A DISCOVERY WHEN HE TRIES TO SORT JOE AVERAGE AMERICANS' TRASH.

HELLO? ANYBODY HOME?!

THE SKINNY-LEGGED STRANGER STEPS IN

FORGET IT! THERE'S NO WAY YOU CAN SORT ALL THAT TRASH BY YOURSELF!

HEAPING LANDFILLS! YOU'RE RIGHT!

WHAT WE NEED IS A WAY TO WAKE THESE PEOPLE UP TO THE NEED FOR RECYCLING!

YEAH! WAKE UP!

TO GET EVERY AMERICAN TO DO THEIR OWN SORTING!

YEAH! OWN SORTING.... OOO AAHH...

SMACK!

OOO! OW!! OUCH OUCH!!

WHAT'S WRONG?! WHAT'S WRONG!?

LEEP

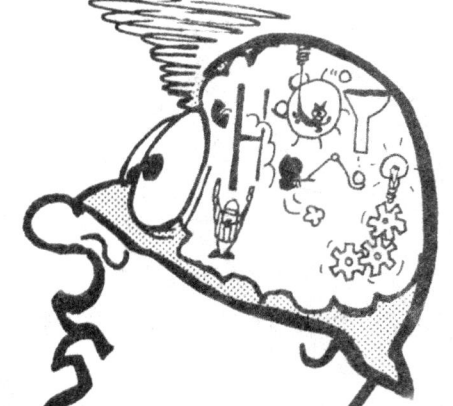

THE WHEELS WERE RUSTY, BUT TURNING.

#53, *Epic Adventure N, May 5, 1990*

CONTINUED FROM LAST WEEK...
THE RECYCLONE HAD AN IDEA.

OOO! OW! OUCH! OUCH!!

AND IMMEDIATELY GOT ON THE HORN!

THE STRANGER WITH THE SKINNY LEGS KNEW THE CLONE WANTED EVERY AMERICAN TO SORT THEIR TRASH FOR RECYCLING, BUT WHAT, YES *WHAT* WAS HE UP TO?!?

A KNOCK SHOOK THE DOOR.

KNOCK.

THERE STOOD ICKEY WOODS, RUNNING BACK FOR THE CINCINNATI BENGALS

AND BUD BIERGUTOWSKI, LEADER OF MILWAUKEE'S HOKEY-POKEY POLKA BAND!

#54, *Epic Adventure O*, May 12, 1990

by LEE P.

CONTINUED...
THE RECYCLONE, ICKEY WOODS AND BUD BIERGUTOWSKI LOCKED THEMSELVES IN A ROOM TO WORK ON A WAY TO GET AMERICA TO RECYCLE. THE STRANGER WITH THE SKINNY LEGS WAS POWERFUL CURIOUS.

WHAT ARE THEY DOING IN THERE WHAT WHAT WHAT WHAT?

ONLY ONCE IN A WEEK DID THE MYSTERIOUS DOOR OPEN

WO BIST DER KLEINE MENSCHEN WATRE KLOSET, BITTE?

THIRD DOOR ON YOUR LEFT.

THEN, ONE DAY...

WE'RE FINISHED!

FINISHED? WITH WHAT?!

IT'S A SIMPLE LITTLE DANCE STEP ABOUT RECYCLING. IT'S CALLED THE "SORTIN' SHUFFLE!"

WELL, SHOW IT TO ME... QUICK!!

COPYRIGHT 1990 LEE P.

WE CAN'T SHOW IT TO YOU *NOW*!

AND WHY NOT?!?

LEEP

WE'VE RUN OUT OF PANELS.

AUGH!

CONTINUED

#55, *Epic Adventure P*, May 19, 1990

#57, *Epic Adventure R*, June 2, 1990

THE RECYCLONE

by LEE P.

THE SMALL BOY REPLACED "THE RECYCLONE'S EPIC ADVENTURE." THE BOOK HAD PRODUCED THE INTENDED EFFECT—HE WAS READY TO SLEEP.

JUNE 2090

HE TRUDGED TO BED, SECURE IN THE HAPPY ENDING OF A 100-YEAR-OLD FAIRY TALE.

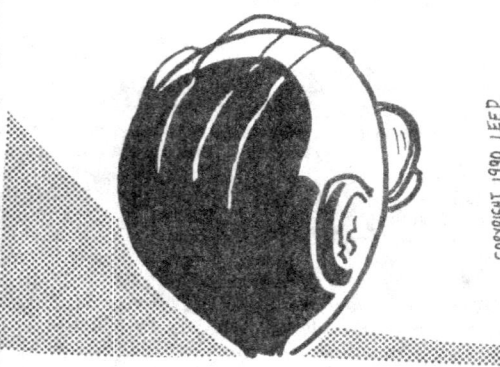

COPYRIGHT 1990 LEE P.

LEEP

BUT WHAT WILL THE WORLD _REALLY_ BE LIKE IN 2090? THAT STORY REMAINS UNWRITTEN, AND WE ARE ITS AUTHORS.

WILL RECYCLING MAKE A DIFFERENCE? WILL THE SORTING SHUFFLE CATCH ON? WILL THE STRANGER WITH THE SKINNY LEGS BE NAMED?

AND SPEAKING OF IDENTITIES, WHO IS THIS KID? WHY DID HE INTRODUCE AND END THE SERIES? HOW IS HE RELATED TO OUR STORY?

WE MAY NEVER FULLY KNOW.

NOT CONTINUED. THIS IS IT. REALLY.

The inside scoop

Inside jokes showed up in several strips. A wild night at a bar called the Crazy Horse provided material for #59. Three Auburn celebrities appeared in *Taking Burt for a Ride*, #60. Martha's popcorn hut sat next to the newspaper office, and was run by Martha Falka for over 50 years. (That's Paul "Doc" Trausch, Martha's frequent popcorn pal, sitting on the bench.) On hot summer nights, the aroma from Martha's Popcorn Stand lured customers from all over town.

The third Auburn institution: Mayor Burt Dickman (the Burt of *Taking Burt for a Ride*, #60). Dickman owned an odd collection of toys in the early 1990's, including a retired city garbage truck. Dickman lent the truck to the grassroots recycling group for the parade mentioned in #25. Only after the parade started did the novice driver learn that the truck did not have brakes.

U
Pun*

Ah, the pun. Last refuge of the lazy joke writer. And bad puns are the easiest of all, as *Recycle Post Haste*, #62, proves.

Twenty-five years ago, newspaper office trash cans overflowed with letters and newsprint. All of this paper went into a dumpster each night. Happily, the Evening Star jumped on the recycling bandwagon early.

Paper recycling has made a huge difference. According to the American Forest and Paper Association, recycling annually recovers over 330 pounds of paper for each American.

* A pun is beneath you

See Paper Recycling Statistics *for yourself*:

www.epa.gov/osw/conserve/materials/paper/faqs.htm

Dropping temperature

"Coolness" repeats as a theme throughout the strips for a reason. Once actors and athletes take up a cause, it's easier to get kids to follow their lead. I hoped that Recyclone could act as a stand-in for a celebrity—an adult figure that kids liked and would follow. If Recyclone made it okay to recycle, as he tries in #61, some of the stigma might be removed.

No longer in the bag

Today we get rid of yard waste with mulching mowers and backyard compost piles. Some communities even offer curbside pickup of sticks and leaves. So it seems illogical that grass and other plant trimmings could cause landfill problems.

But 25 years ago, sticks, twigs and grass clippings went in the garbage can, as reported in *Clip Waste in the Grass*, #65.

#58, *Think Again, Bucko!*, June 23, 1990

#59, *Crazy Horse*, July 2, 1990

CLONE, HERE, NOT FEELING TOO WELL AFTER STAYING OUT LATE LAST NIGHT CELEBRATING AN *OLD* FRIEND'S BIRTHDAY.

WHEN I DON'T FEEL WELL, I GET CRANKY. AND WHEN I GET CRANKY, I SAY WHAT'S ON MY MIND.

LEEP

RECYCLING WORKS, DANG IT, AND IF EVERYBODY SORTED NEWSPAPERS, BOTTLES AND CANS OUT OF THEIR TRASH, LANDFILLS WOULD BE SPARED, ENERGY SAVED AND THE WHOLE DARN EARTH WOULD BE A LITTLE GREENER AND A LOT LESS POO-POO!

WHAT?

OH! I AM SORRY, YOUR-ROYAL-HAPPY-BIRTHDAY-HIGHNESS, IF I OFFENDED YOU! PLEASE EXCUSE MY FRANKNESS!!

ED. NOTE – LAST NIGHT WILLOUGHBY WAS ONE CRAZY HORSE!

FRANKNESS, SCHMANKNESS! IT'S YOUR BREATH THAT'S OFFENSIVE!

#60, *Taking Burt for a Ride*, July 14, 1990

CLONE, HERE! A GRAND AND NOBLE EXPERIMENT BEGINS IN AUBURN NEXT WEEK!

PLASTIC RECEPTACLES SUCH AS THESE HAVE BEEN DISTRIBUTED TO SELECTED CITY HOMES.

HOMEOWNERS HAVE BEEN ASKED TO SORT NEWSPAPERS, BOTTLES, CANS AND PLASTICS OUT OF THEIR TRASH AND PLACE THEM IN AFOREMENTIONED RECEPTACLES.

ED. NOTE: DOMESTIC ENGINEER PORTRAYED BY MOONBEAM.

THEREAFTERLY ONCE PER WEEK A CITY EMPLOYEE (NO, NOT YOU, BURT!) WILL EMPTY THE RECEPTACLES RIGHT AT THE HOMEOWNERS CURBSIDE!

IF RESPONSE TO THE EXPERIMENT IS POSITIVE, THE PROGRAM *COULD* EXPAND TO INCLUDE THE WHOLE CITY!

RESPONSE-O-METER

POSITIVE

NEGATIVE

ANY QUESTIONS?

CAN I RIDE ON THE COLLECTION TRUCK?

ME, TOO!

#62, *Recycle Post Haste*, July 28, 1990

#64, *Tight Spot*, August 11, 1990

#65, *Clip Waste in the Grass,* **August 18, 1990**

Arise, Zombies, and Reduce!

After *Plight of the Shopping Dead*, #70, appeared, the Pennsylvania Resource Council called. They very nicely pointed out that they were a local resource, not a national one. So would Recyclone ask Indiana residents to please quit calling?

An update is in order. The website below explains the over packaging problem well and offers some suggestions.

So Help Me, Who?

Each stage show ended with Recyclone leading the audience in the 3-R Pledge. To do the pledge correctly, pledgees wiggled three fingers on their right hand, as shown in #71.

The popularity of Teenage Mutant Ninja Turtles began to wane, so in later shows the last line became, ".... So help me, Al Gore."

See **Packaging Suggestions** *for yourself:*

www.greenchoices.org/green-living/food-drink/packaging

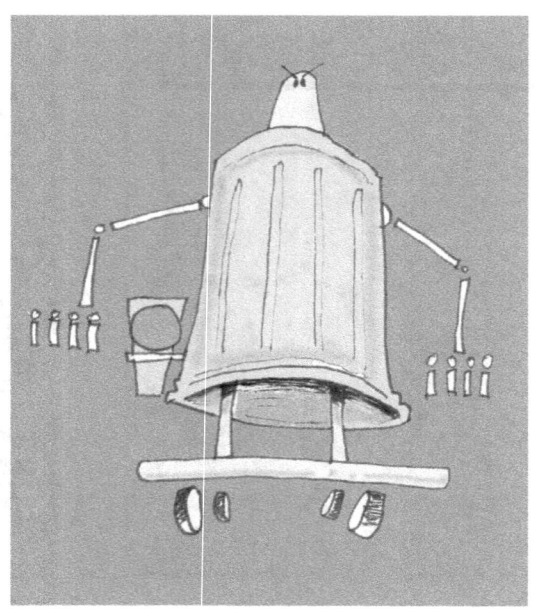

Robo Reducer

Robo Reducer to the Rescue

Number 72 introduces Robo Reducer, a recycling robot.

His body: an upside-down trash can.

His head: a tin can.

His legs: shopping-cart wheels.

His weapon: a modified grocery store clerk's price gun capable of reducing over packaging.

#67, *Mother of All Critics*, September 8, 1990

#68, *Plastic vs. Plastic*, September 15, 1990

#69, *Cash for Trash*, September 22, 1990

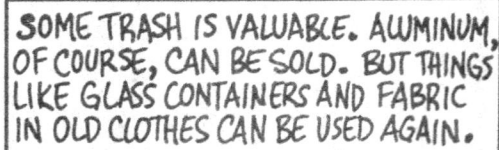

#70, *Plight of the Shopping Dead*, September 29, 1990

#71, *So Help Me, Turtles*, October 9, 1990

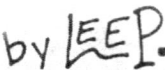

#72, *Introducing Robo Reducer*, October 11, 1990

Less is more

My Great Aunt Emma Krueger of Wittenberg, WI, played a recurring role in my life. It was just natural that, whenever I needed an old-fashioned-sounding name in the cartoon world, I turned to Em and her friends. (*One, Two, Shut the Flue, #75*)

Aunt Em Kruger

Em grew up on a farm and lived through the Great Depression. She and other Wittenbergers of her generation practiced the 3-R's *WAY* before anyone coined the term "3-R's." For instance, Em used only one pan of dishwater during a day. Then at night, she threw the pan of water into the toilet to flush away a day's worth of accumulated waste. Em also saved every food container. She collected so many that, when you opened her cabinet doors, an avalanche of jelly jars and butter tubs came raining down.

I viewed some of Em's saintly saving with a cynical eye. There seemed to me to be competition between Em and her friends over whom could live most modestly.

For instance, Em left strict instructions that, should she pass onto a better world in winter, under no circumstances should heat be turned on in church. Just so you know, a church with low heat on a cold, Wisconsin day would be a mighty uncomfortable place for the living. Folks would notice. It would be the talk of the town.

Recognize the irony? Getting noticed for living modestly?

Quick notes

• Hey, I can evolve. *Politically Incorrect Reducing*, #76, strikes me as insensitive. I wouldn't use such a cheap gag today.

• Every cartoonist of my generation is obligated to take a stab at "Mad Magazine." I mailed #77 *Mad Garbologist* to the publication, but never heard from them.

• Garbologist is a great word. It's fun to say; Garbologist, garbologist, garbologist.

• *Sing Your Troubles Away*, #80, counts among my personal favorites. It captures the goofy nature of Recyclone.

#73, *If*, October 13, 1990

by LEE P.

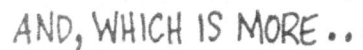

#74, *Lighten Your Load*, October 27, 1990

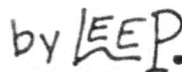

YOU MAY BE ASKING YOURSELF: JUST WHAT THE HECK IS GOING ON, HERE?

WELL, EVERY YEAR AMERICA PRODUCES AN AVERAGE OF 1,500 POUNDS OF TRASH FOR EVERY MAN, WOMAN AND CHILD IN THE COUNTRY!!

BY RECYCLING, YOU LESSEN YOUR INDIVIDUAL LOAD AND TAKE THE WEIGHT OFF FUTURE GENERATIONS!

SO, YOU SEE, RECYCLING MAKES SENSE EVEN IF BARYSHNIKOV HERE DOESN'T!

TA DA!!

#75, *One, Two, Shut the Flue!*, November 3, 1990

#76, *Politically Incorrect Reducing,* November 17, 1990

#77, *Mad Garbologist*, December 3, 1990

#78, *Warning Signs*, December 8, 1990

TODAY, FOR A BREAK FROM THE RECYCLONE'S SILLINESS, WE PRESENT A SELECTION OF WARNING SIGNS AND ASK YOU TO PONDER WHAT STEPS YOU MIGHT TAKE TO AVOID CATASTROPHE.

COPYRIGHT 1990 LEEP

#79, *Robo Reducer to the Rescue*, December 15, 1990

THE PEOPLE STOOD HELPLESS BEFORE AN EVER GROWING MENACE. FROM WHENCE WOULD THEIR HELP COME? (THAT'S RIGHT- *WHENCE!*)

WHEN OUT OF THE HILLS CAME A GALVANIZED STRANGER WHO WAS PACKING A PECULIAR LOOKING PISTOL!

"NEVER FEAR, GOOD PEOPLE!" HE SAID IN A TINNY VOICE. "BY REDUCING OVERPACKAGING, WE CAN CUT THE AMOUNT OF TRASH HEADED FOR LANDFILL!"

THEN HE PULLED HIS PISTOL. "DIE, UNNECESSARY TRASH, DIE!" HE SHOUTED, AND THE AIR FILLED WITH PLASTIC PLASMA AND CARDBOARD GUTS.

"HOORAY!" SAID THE PEOPLE WHEN THE MONSTROUS TRASH HAD BEEN REDUCED TO A MANAGEABLE SIZE. NO ONE NOTICED THE LONE STRANGER TAKE A POWDER.

HAR HAR HAR HAR

HI, HO WHEEL BEARINGS! AWAAAAY!!!

DADDY, WHO WAS THAT UPSIDE-DOWN TRASH CAN?

SON, I DON'T HAVE THE FOGGIEST IDEA.

#80, *Sing Your Troubles Away,* **December 22, 1990**

#81, *Keep Trash on the Run*, December 29, 1990

Altering consciousness

Jimmy Swaggart appeared on front pages in the 1990's. Remember him? A slick haired TV preacher with tears streaming down his cheeks? Swaggart cried a lot after being caught in a scandal with a prostitute.

I would be reluctant to buy a used car from Swaggart. I certainly didn't believe he owned special insight into the mysteries of life. But Jimmy inspired me in one way. You can see the result in *Environmental Evangelist*, #82.

Rocky Reasons

Sylvester Stallone made a career out of the Rocky Balboa series of movies. *Rocky V* went onscreen in 1990.

As a fighter, *Rocky Reasons*, #91, compares to Rocky Balboa in one significant way: they've both taken too many hits to the head.

Enveloping Over Packaging

The Evening Star received an armful of mail each day. (*Enveloping An Overpackaging Problem*, #86.) Reporters took turns going through the pile.

Picking out significant pieces took a few seconds—you looked for handwriting. This showed a real person behind the letter. On a good day, the newspaper might receive three or four personal pieces of mail.

Mass mailings made up a good portion of the armful of mail. Organizations across the country included every newspaper in the U.S. on their press release mailing lists. Why? On the off chance that a reporter might take an interest and do a story. Press releases of importance might be in the mix, but a high percentage contained nothing of interest to our area. For instance, our Indiana office might receive a press release from California raisin growers, announcing that they harvested a record yield.

The greatest percentage of the armful of mail went straight in the trash. Why? Advertising. The newspaper would not do a story on a product made for profit. Whether ignorant of this fact or simply because they didn't care, manufacturers kept mailing ads. There seemed to be no consideration of the waste involved.

Automotive manufacturers proved the worst offenders. They sent packages by overnight delivery (to emphasize the material was important) stuffed with three-ring binders. The binders burst with ads posing as press releases, glossy color photos, even plastic sleeves of slides. Just the printing and mailing cost must have topped $75 per piece—and that didn't include the cost of production.

Before Recyclone, these big binders went in the trash. After Recyclone, guilt drove me to take action. I recycled what I could and reused the rest.

#82, *Environmental Evangelist*, January 5, 1991

#83, *Germ of an Idea*, January 12, 1991

#85, *HELP!*, January 19, 1991

#86, *Enveloping an Over Packaging Problem*, February 9, 1991

#87, *Pucker Up and Recycle*, February 16, 1991

#88, *Pie in the Sky*, February 23, 1991

#89, *Laundromat Encounter,* March 2, 1991

#90, *Herr Kahnschtomper*, March 9, 1991

#91, *Rocky Reasons*, March 15, 1991

#93*, *Hoppy Easter,* **March 30, 1991**

*This strip is shown out of order so that *The Big Cal Series* can be presented in uninterrupted sequence.

The Untrashables

Recyclone tells his second continuing story in *The Big Cal Series*, #92-102.

The villain, Big Cal, represents the excess of the 1980's. His flabby body useless, he relies on a mechanical contraption to keep him upright, move him from place to place, even keep his eyelids open.

Recyclone recruited kids who vowed to fight waste. He called them "The Untrashables."

Aren't most of life's big problems in reality lots of little problems? That's certainly true of wastefulness. It happens one house, one thermostat, one trash can at a time. Hence, by commiting lots of little, wasteful acts, Big Cal's henchmen give Recyclone one big headache.

Our Superhero's solution to the little problems fits his core mission: to enlist children in the fight against waste.

I modeled The Untrashables on The Untouchables. During Prohibition in the 1930's, United States law made it illegal to sell booze and beer. In Chicago, Al Capone and his gang broke the law and fought with other gangsters. They succeeded for a long time because Chicago law officers accepted bribes in exchange for looking the other way. Then United States agents arrived. They could not be bribed. People called them The Untouchables.

In the same way, The Untrashables won't go back on their pledge to fight waste.

#94, *Big Cal B*, April 6, 1991

#96, *Big Cal D*, May 11, 1991

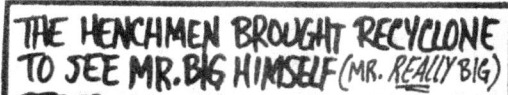

#98, *Big Cal F*, May 25, 1991

THE RECYCLONE SUBDUED BIG CAL WITH HIS HOPE AND OPTIMISM.

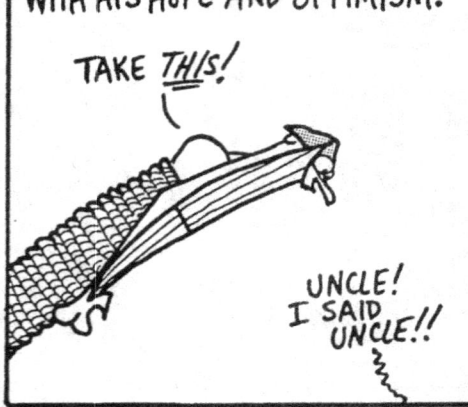

THEN, AS IN ALL GOOD-BEATS-BAD STORIES, BIG CAL ASKED RECYCLONE TO EXPLAIN HIS SUCCESS.

AS YOUR HENCHMEN SHOWED ME OBSTACLES TO THE ENVIRONMENTAL MOVEMENT...

AND THEIR ATTITUDES TOWARDS RECYCLING MADE ME SMILE!

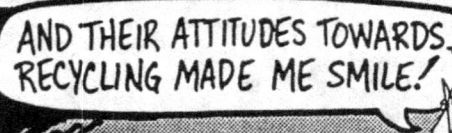

#99, *Big Cal G*, June 1, 1991

WHEN BIG CAL'S PLAN BACKFIRED, THE RECYCLONE ASSERTED HIMSELF LIKE THE SUPERHERO HE IS...

HELP ME OUT OF THIS ROPE, WILL YA?

IT'S YARN.

EVEN THOUGH BIG CAL HAD BEEN REDUCED TO A SHADOW OF THE GODFATHER OF CONSUMPTION WHO RULED THE 1980s...

PRETTY LARGE SHADOW, HUH?

THE PROBLEM OF HIS HENCHMAN REMAINED.

WHAT?

TAP TAP TAP

FOR EVERYWHERE THE LITTLE BUGGERS WERE WASTING THE ENVIRONMENT.

PSSST...

CLICK!

THE RECYCLONE NEEDED A PLAN.

THINK, RECYCLONE, THINK!!

OOO!

OW!

OW!

OUCHIE!

OOO!

LEEP. © 1991

#100, *Big Cal H*, June 8, 1991

#101, *Big Cal I*, June 17, 1991

THE RECYCLONE

by LEE P.

THE RECYCLONE IS LOOKING FOR A FEW GOOD CHILDREN!

CHILDREN WITH ALUMINUM IN THEIR SOULS, GLASS-LIKE CLARITY IN THEIR VISION, AND NEWSPAPERS PILING UP IN THEIR GARAGES.

CHILDREN WITH THE 3-R STUFF TO BE *UNTRASHABLES!!*

RECYCLE REDUCE REUSE

IF *YOU* WANT TO BECOME AN UNTRASHABLE, WRITE ON A SHEET OF PAPER: "I WANNA ARREST WASTE." AND SIGN YOUR NAME.

(INCLUDE YOUR OWN DRAWING, IF YOU WISH)

MAIL OR DELIVER THE PAPER TO RECYCLONE, % THE EVENING STAR, 118 W. NINTH ST., AUBURN, IND., 46706

LEE P. © 1991

IF YOUR PAPER ARRIVES BY NOON OF THURSDAY, JUNE 20, YOUR NAME WILL APPEAR RIGHT HERE NEXT SATURDAY!!

WELL, NOT RIGHT HERE *EXACTLY*, BUT IN *NEXT* WEEK'S EDITION OF THE STAR, GOT IT?

THE RECYCLONE by LEE P.

AN **UNTRASHABLE** IS...

THE UNTRASHABLES ARE:

CORY MILLER, LEWIS PARK
STEVEN N. MINNICH, KAMI RATHBURN
TONYA CZAJA, CARLY GALLIGHER
LAURA HUNDAGEN, JO KING
JA DA WARSTLER, SARAH TRUBEY
VANESSA WEIMER, ANN FRIEND
ANGELA FULEKI, GREG BOZARTH
RYAN SONNENBERG, TIM SPILLERS
JAMIACA SNYDER, JOSH GROGG
HEATHER BURNS, CHRIS FRIEND
AUTUMN BONECUTTER, ROBYN RINGLER
HEATHER FORE, MALISSA WILDES
SARAH RECKER, MARIA RECKER
KATHY WILDES, JENNY WILDES
HEATHER SHEARER, JAKE MYERS
LINDSAY BISHOP, ALISON BERCAW
BREE C. SHEW, RACHAEL FULEKI
JANA VERHAGE, SARAH HUNDAGEN
KATIE KADUK, BRANT REYNOLDS
BILLY ELLIOTT, KELLY ELLIOTT
JEREMY PRENTICE, KATIE KING
DAWN PRENTICE, JILL FARLOW
ERIN MARIE FARLOW, AMY WEILER
ADAM EMERSON, AMBER BERGDALL
DANE MILLER, JACQUELYN BERCAW
DANNY FLEMING, BRITNEY FUENTES
JOSH KESSLER, JESSICA LAMPE
STEPHANIE MINNICH, TYLER MOORE
JESSICA YOHO, SHANE SONNENBERG
BENJAMIN WARSTLER, MOLLY WEILER
TROY WEIMER, NATHEN WOLF
JONATHAN HINES, KATHY BERGDALL
JUDY COLANDINO, JENNY RECKER
BRANDON SILVERS, CHRISTIE MYERS
WENDY SHIRER, JESSICA DAVIS, KIRA DEPEW
KEVIN GALLIGHER, JACKIE RECKER
MICHAEL RECKER, BRIAN KESSLER
AMY TROVINGER, BRITANNY REYNOLDS
CONNIE MYERS, CAROL SIGLER, MARK TROVINGER, BROOKE CREAGER, MICHAEL ALLEN KING, + BOO

CLEANLY

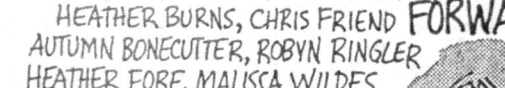

FORWARD LOOKING

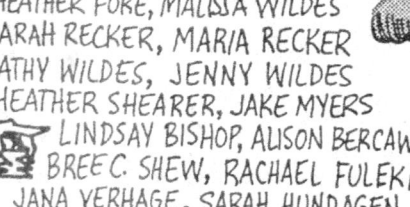

TRUSTWORTHY

BELOVED

ON TOP OF THE WORLD!!

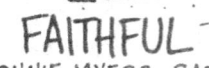

FAITHFUL

Where ideas come from

Inspiration comes from many corners. I admire the work of old cartoonists. At the time of *High Wire Act*, #103 and *Muddy Bottom Bother*, #113, I was reading "We have met the enemy and he is us," by Walt Kelly. Cartoonist Rube Goldberg liked to draw unlikely and needlessly complicated. inventions. I tried to be Goldbergian in *3-R Fireworks*, #104.

Ray Charles, the blind blues singer, made a series of commercials for Diet Pepsi in the early 1990's. *Ah-hah!*, #105, imitates Ray and his backup singers.

See Walt Kelly artwork *for yourself:*
www.bpib.com/kelly.htm

See a Rube Goldberg Invention *for yourself:*
www.rubegoldberg.com/gallery

See a Ray Charles' commercial *for yourself:*
www.youtube.com/watch?v=3D_srHpH6jg

Anyone can recycle

If you haven't caught on, Recyclone's main message is that you don't have to be a superhero to recycle. Everyone can help save the earth, as in *Superpowers Not Needed*, #112.

Auburn autos sold at auction

Folks who live outside Indiana connect the town of Auburn to its annual Auburn-Cord-Duesenberg Festival. The Auburn Automobile Company made national headlines in the 1920's and 1930's. The company broke apart in the late stages of the Great Depression, but its stylish and innovative automobiles remain objects of interest. Every year auto enthusiasts gather in Auburn to reminisce.

For many years, the Kruse Auction took place at the same time as the festival. Kruse auctioned off cars of all vintages, which attracted buyers from around the world. The auction inspired *Auctioning Our Future*, #110.

Driving a million-dollar, 1920's Duesenberg? Now, that's reusing with style!

Andy's ice cream

In an episode of the Andy Griffith Show, "The Sermon for Today," Andy and Barney sit on a porch swing on a hot summer day. Andy says to Barney, "You know what I believe I'll do? Run down to the drugstore and get some ice cream for later," Barney says he'll go along.

Then, they both just sit there.

That scene is probably not as funny in today's manic-paced world, but I've always loved it. So I tried to recreate it in *3-R Dog Days*, #106.

#103, *High Wire Act*, June 29, 1991

#105, *Recycling Works, Ah-Hah!*, July 13, 1991

#106, *Dog Days*, July 20, 1991

#107, *Fishing for Recyclables,* July 27, 1991

#108, *Old McClone*, August 9, 1991

#109, *When in Doubt, Form a Committee*, August 17, 1991

#110, *Auctioning Our Future*, August 31, 1991

#111, *It's in the Bag,* **September 7, 1991**

#112, *Superpowers Not Needed,* **September 14, 1991**

#113, *Muddy Bottom Bother,* **September 21, 1991**

#114, *Testing the Wind*, September 29, 1991

#115, *Don't Trust the Monkey,* **October 5, 1991**

#116, *Al Apathy*, October 26, 1991

#118, *Which Way Do We Go?*, December 7, 1991

#119, *Naughty Or Nice?*, December 14, 1991

Celebrity rise and fall

Reading *Resolutions We'd Like to See*, #120, you might conclude that being known by only one name provides staying power. Oprah and Madonna remain in the public mind, although both have lost the influence they enjoyed in the 1990's.

Meanwhile, being a politician will get your name in the history books, but may not lead to lasting fame. George H.W. Bush and Mikhail Gorbachev led superpower nations, but kids today don't know who they are.

Poor Michael Jackson. He rose the highest and fell the farthest.

Top Ten Lists

Cool people watched David Letterman on late night TV in 1992. His Top Ten Lists were widely praised and imitated, as Recyclone did in *Top Ten Reasons to Recycle*, #122.

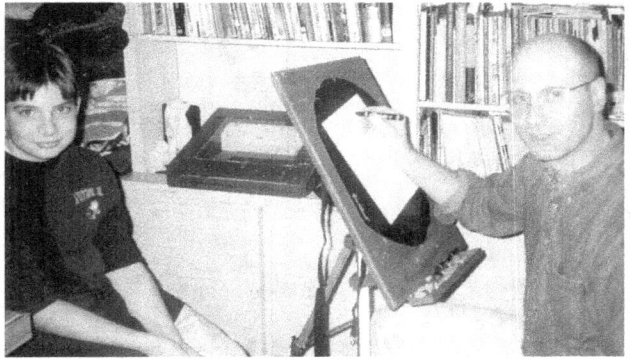

Smile, Kyle__I served as mentor to Twelve-year-old Kyle Morris of Huntertown through the "Peak Into the Future" program. Kyle visited the office and got his cartoon, *Kyle Takes a Turn*, #126, published in the Star.

This is the earth in trouble . . .

A TV ad from the 1990's shows a man standing near a stove and hot frying pan. The man picks up an egg and says, "This is your brain." He points to the frying pan. "This is drugs." He cracks the egg into the pan; the egg turns white and bubbling hot. The man says, "This is your brain on drugs."

Pretty effective. I try for the same impact in #127, *Any Questions?*

Is the analogy between drugs and wastefulness a stretch? I don't think so. Americans have been addicted to natural resources since the beginning of the country. And, for just as long, there have been people who denied the obvious—our actions hurt the earth and it may never recover.

See **"Any Questions?" ad** *for yourself:*
www.youtube.com/watch?v=ub_a2t0ZfTs

See **Americans' Global Warning Beliefs** *for yourself:*
environment.yale,edu/climate-communication/files/Climate-Beliefs-September-2012.pdf

#120, *Resolutions We'd Like to See,* **January 4, 1992**

#121, *Recycling Workout*, January 18, 1992

#122, *Top Ten Reasons to Recycle*, January 25, 1992

#124, *Every Day, Except ..., February 15, 1992*

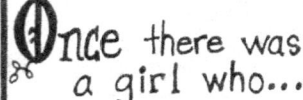  

#125, *O, Give Me a Recycling Home*, February 22, 1992

#126, *Kyle Takes a Turn*, March 7, 1992

#127, *Any Questions?*, March 14, 1992

#128, *March Madness,* **March 28, 1992**

THE RECYCLONE BREAKS INTO THE OPEN!

HE GIVES A DEFENDER HIS PATENTED SPIN MOVE!

HE JUMPS COMPLETELY OVER THE OTHER TEAM!

Wayne's world is a clean world

Before the Austin Powers movies, comedian Mike Myers built his reputation on characters created for the TV show *Saturday Night Live*. The skit "Wayne's World" featured two Chicago suburban teenagers who starred in their own cable show.

Wayne and Garth popularized camera shots such as "unnecessary zoom" and "extreme close up." Their catch phrase "NOT!" exposed false information.

Recyclone partied on as DeWorld and Moonbeam as Gearth in *It's a Clean World*, #129.

See Wayne's World *for yourself:*
www.nbc.com/saturday-night-live/video/waynes-world/n9871

#129, *It's a Clean World*, April 4, 1992

#130, *Home Energy Saving Guide,* April 16, 1992

#131, *Wake-Up Call,* **June 6, 1992**

#132, *The Sword Hanging Over Us*, February 22, 1992

#133, *Prodding Us Forward*, July 11, 1992

Extra art

These drawings were printed on t-shirts or used in print ads. The drawing at top right is a knock-off of a Mountain Dew ad from the early 1990's.

Graphic novels

The last Recyclone cartoon, *Prodding Us Forward*, #133, ran July 11, 1992.

I don't recall the exact reason I stopped drawing the strips, but my personal life got busy. I married in May of 1993. In August, my bride and I left for an extended visit to Alaska. When we returned to Indiana, the Star assigned me to Steuben County.

And, at the end of 1993, we moved from Auburn to Steuben's county seat, Angola.

I certainly didn't forget Recyclone. As I said at the beginning of this book, I continued to do shows with him until 2000. And I continued to revisit him in different formats.

At least twice, I tried to tell Recyclone's story in graphic novels. I found the following sketches in my files . . .

empty

Moonbeam runs to the recycling center. She meets Recyclone and they talk. Darla, Moonbeam's foster sister, Sh... llows, but she is not happy

HANDLER ...WHEN YOU ADD IT ALL UP, THAT'S 1.45 *BILLION* POUNDS OF TRASH!

WOW! TO SAVE THE EARTH, WE HAVE TO WIN LOTS OF SMALL BATTLES!

I'M BATTLING BOREDOM ALREADY!

EXCUSE ME, MISTER, TO SAVE THE EARTH YOU MUST BEGIN BY BATTLING IGNORANCE!

BATTLE IGNORANCE—THAT'S DUMB!

WHY BATTLE IGNORANCE?

BECAUSE HE'S RIGHT BEHIND YOU!

LOOK OUT!

BAM!

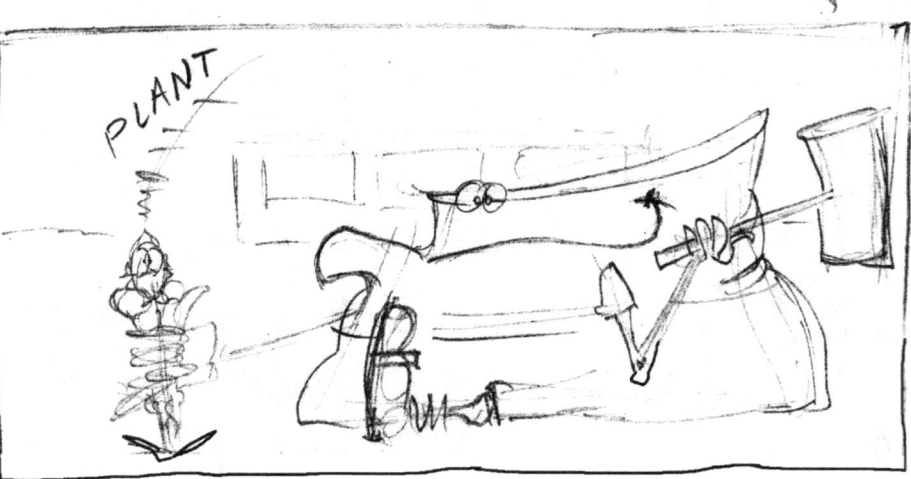

MOONELAM DECIDES IT IS UP TO HER TO DEFEAT IGNORANCE.

WHAT CAN ONE KID DO? THINK THINK THINK THINK THINK THINK

THAT'S IT! SNAP! I'LL MAKE HIM **THINK!**

HEY, YOU! HOW MUCH TRASH DOES THE AVERAGE AMERICAN THROW AWAY EACH DAY?

HUH?

LOOK! THE LITTLE GIRL IS TRYING TO CONFUSE HIM!

JUST LIKE OUR READERS!

COME ON, I'M WAITING FOR AN ANSWER!

HMM! HMM!

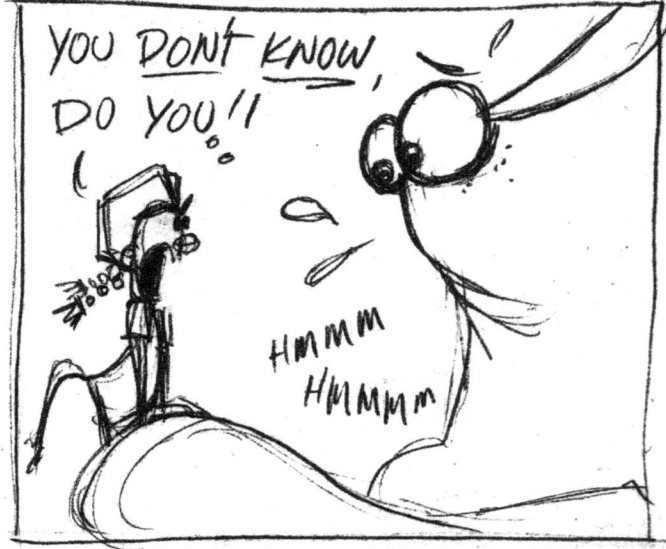

YOU _DON'T KNOW_, DO YOU?!

HMMM HMMMM

WELL, MOONBEAM KEPT BATTLING IGNORANCE WITH WHAT SHE HAD LEARNED FROM RECYCLONE, AND IGNORANCE KEPT KICKING HIMSELF FOR NOT KNOWING BETTER, UNTIL...

KICK
KICK
ICK

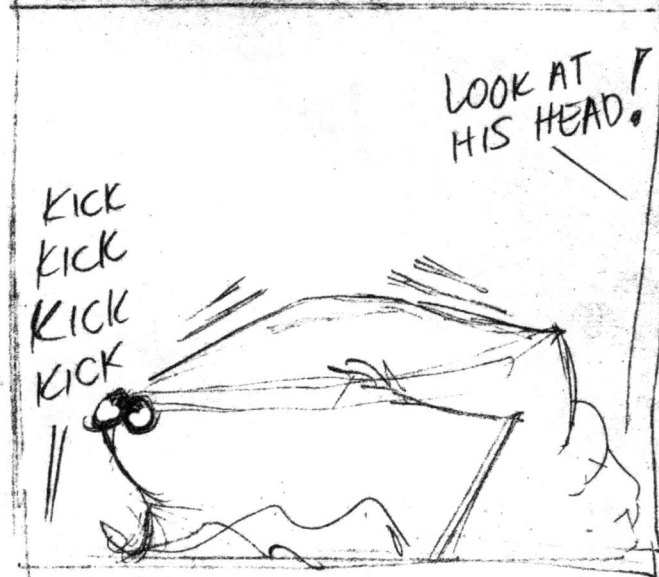

KICK
KICK
KICK
KICK

LOOK AT HIS HEAD!

POP!

IT'S POPPING BACK INTO SHAPE!

HUH?

AH! THAT IS EVER SO MUCH BETTER!

HE'S SMART NOW!

NOT "SMART." *INFORMED.*

THAT'S RIGHT! MOST PEOPLE WHO HARM THE EARTH ARE *NOT* STUPID, THEY JUST DON'T KNOW ANY BETTER!

OR DON'T CARE

THE CUBS WILL WIN THE PENNANT!

Multi-media

Some things are better left forgotten.

In my files, I found scripts for a series of television shows starring Recyclone. A date of June 21, 1994, appears on the front. I tried to involve my family in the project. The scripts lists my brother, Joel, his wife, Ellen, and their daughter, Alex, as cast members.

I also found a video script. This project came closer to being realized. A local video team approached me about collaborating on a series of how-to-draw instructional videos. We talked of many similar collaborations, including a video starring Recyclone. We shot the first how-to-draw show. Only editing needed to be done to complete the video. But the partner responsible never got around to it. So the collaboration ended after one unfinished project.

Part of the blame must be attributed to unrealistic expectations. I plan elaborate productions that require impractical amounts of time and work.

For example, a local cable station asked Recyclone to star in some public service announcement ads. I worked on a script for days. The script called for several characters, multiple camera angles, close ups, animation. On the day of the shoot, I explained my vision to the production crew, which consisted of one guy with a hand-held camera and a young woman with a clipboard. They both looked at me blankly.

Have you seen *The Office* episode in which Michael planned an elaborate commercial while the professional production crew wanted only one shot of the office employees waving? It was kind of like that.

I put my script away. The cable station production crew and I compromised.

In other words, we shot a single, straight head-and-shoulders view of Recyclone as he looked directly into the camera. The entire recording session took 10 minutes.

Chapter books for children

Along with graphic novels, I told Recyclone's story through more conventional children's chapter books.

Well, almost conventional.

When in 2003 I began writing the novel from which the following excerpt was taken, I was reading *Tristam Shandy*. This early novel reads like a roller coaster. It stops, starts, goes sideways, follows new paths, turns upside down.

It's quite a ride.

You never heard of *Tristam Shandy*? Don't feel bad. The author, Laurence Sterne, died almost 250 years ago. He published *Tristam Shandy* in 1759.

You've probably heard of Lemony Snicket and *A Series of Unfortunate Events*. Daniel Handler wrote the series of books in 1999 and 2000. I must have been reading these books also, for in re-reading this excerpt, I notice their influence as well.

Anyhoo, back to our story: I wrote two novels in which children save the earth from wasteful-ness. Both novels star Moonbeam as the main character. And both novels include a huge monster, along the lines of the Bulk Trash Dragon, as the villain.

Recyclone appears in the first novel, but he is left out of the second.

For that reason, I chose to share the first chapter of the first book, titled, *Wuwwuw*. (Wuwwuw stands for What You Want, When You Want It.)

Wuwwuw by Lee P. Sauer

Chapter One

The Monster

A shadowy figure walked down a suburban sidewalk. The figure appeared to be that of

a young girl. She wore an unfashionably short trench coat and sunglasses. Her hair would not

get in her eyes.

How do I know this?

Her hair was pulled tight into pigtails.

A year ago, the suburb through which the sidewalk ran had been a cornfield. On this day,

new houses sat on unnaturally green lawns that stretched into the distance.

A boy riding a scooter came down the sidewalk, toward the girl. To let the scooter pass,

the girl—who had incredibly skinny legs—stepped into unnaturally green grass.

"Nerd," growled the boy as he passed. He did not look up.

The girl turned to watch him grow smaller and smaller.

"What is this?" said a voice.

The girl looked. The voice seemed to come from a canary yellow SUV. SUV stands for

Sport Utility Vehicle. The girl knew what SUV stood for, but she didn't know big, gas-guzzling vehicles could talk. When she tilted her head, the girl saw that the voice did not come from the

SUV, but from a man standing in front of the vehicle, inside a garage. The man held a broom in

one hand and what looked like a hairy, old rope in the other.

"Don't know, don't care," said a second voice. The girl shifted. She saw a woman

standing near the man and bent over a cardboard box.

"Well, what should I do with it?" The man sounded peevish.

"Throw it out," said the woman. She picked up the box and moved to the other side of the

garage. "Like I always say, 'wuwwuw.'"

"Right," said the man, looking at the thing in his hand. "Wuwwuw."

He took a step toward the trash can. The thing slipped through his hand.

"What the . . . ?" He picked up the thing and gave it a tug. "It's attached to something."

He looked toward the woman for a reaction. She ignored him.

The man pulled hard. He gained a foot or two of length. He pulled again. Hand over hand,

he began to drag the hairy rope toward himself. Soon, a tangled pile lay at his feet.

The girl noticed that the rope slowly grew in diameter.

"Hee! Hee!" laughed the man, leaning back and throwing his weight into the effort.

"Look at this," he shouted to the woman's back. "There's no end.

"This could go on and on forever!"

Whatever you do, don't stop here. Keep reading.

A gaggle of turkey vultures shook their wings and wheeled into the air. Flying in circles, they kept their eyes on the movement on the ground. It was this movement that had startled them into flight.

A gaggle is a group of birds. In this particular case, a group of very stupid birds.

The object that looked like an old, ever-thicker, hairy rope made a scraping sound as it moved in tiny jerks along the oily earth. If the turkey buzzards had bigger brains, they might have wondered where the object came from and where it was going. If the turkey buzzards had wondered this, they would have realized that they had a bird's eye view from which they could see both.

From high up in the air, even while flying in circles, a smart turkey buzzard would have been able to deduce that the the hairy object came to an end in a suburban garage. Looking toward the other end, an intelligent turkey buzzard would have deduced that the hairy object began in huge piles of trash, around which black pools of ooze bubbled and popped, and from which dirty smoke curled lazily into the sky.

Deduce means "to arrive at a fact by thinking."

A very curious and very smart turkey vulture might have flown close enough to the area from which the hairy object came in order to read the sign. If the turkey vulture recognized letters, it would have learned that this is what the sign said:

Landfill.

In fact, one turkey buzzard did look toward where the hairy object began. Since it was not very smart, the turkey buzzard did not notice the trash or pools or smoke or sign, but it did notice something that interested it's teeny, tiny brain very much.

Rats.

The turkey vulture wheeled toward the landfill. His fellow, small-brained birds followed. They watched the movement and rats on the ground for quite some time.

Then, after several violent jerks, the movement stopped. The rats sniffed the dirty air and quickly disappeared. All was quiet.

Suddenly, the dark mountains of trash rippled. Great clouds of smoke billowed into the sky. The turkey vultures flapped frantically away as a sinister silhouette revealed the source of the smoke to be two, great nostils.

And, as the silhouette grew in height and sinisterality, two red, angry eyes opened.

What does sinisterality mean? I don't know. I just made the word up.

Back on the ground, inside a suburban garage, a man cursed. And outside the garage, hidden behind a canary yellow SUV, a young girl with sunglasses and pigtails flexed her incredibly skinny legs, checked for scooters, and quickly walked away.

Are you scared yet?

You should be.

Heavenly brush with the Big Time

A nice, old guy would regularly stop me on Auburn streets. He'd tell me how much he enjoyed Recyclone comics. Other than recognizing his face and first name, I knew nothing about the man.

One day, this guy called and asked if we could meet. He said he had something important to ask me.

We met.

The nice, old guy told me he was a member of some board for MacDonald's, the national restaurant chain. He was going to Chicago that weekend for a meeting. Could he recommend to the board that MacDonald's use Recyclone to promote recycling?

Sure, I said.

I tried not to get excited. I didn't have any reason not to believe the guy, but it seemed too good to be true. Doubts ran through my mind. Had I misunderstood or misinterpreted him? Did he really have any power? Did he have the ear of decision makers?

I even doubted the guy's sanity. Could he have been making this whole thing up?

Despite the doubts, I was dying with curiousity. Okay, maybe that's a poor choice of words, but I wanted to know what happened at the meeting.

The weekend passed. The nice, old guy didn't call on Monday. Or Tuesday. Finally, about the middle of the week, I called him.

The old guy's wife answered. Sorry, she said, but her husband couldn't come to the phone.

He passed away on Friday.

I can't prove any of this. At the time, I was so shocked I didn't think of investigating further. There's nothing in my files about the old guy. No piece of paper ever changed hands. Today I can't even remember his name. All that remains is a vague memory of the old guy, the meeting and the feelings at learning of his death.

But it makes a good story, doesn't it?

Twentieth Anniversary Book

For the 20th anniversary of the Recyclone comic strip, I began a book much like this one. It contained all of the comics. But, in addition, it introduced new characters and told a new story.

I based the new characters and story on political events at that time. 2008 was an election year. It marked the end of George W. Bush's administration and the beginning of Barack Obama's.

To me, Donald Rumsfeld represented the attitude of the Bush administration. In press conferences, he adjusted his glasses, squinted his eyes and looked down his nose at reporters. His expression seemed to say, "How could anyone so stupid dare to ask ME a question."

In the 20th anniversary book, a character named Ronald Dumsfeld narrates from a podium in the West Wing. Dumsfeld officiates at a memorial service for Recyclone. His message: Recyclone and efforts to battle waste are dead. To highlight the futility of recycling, Dumsfeld shows Recyclone cartoons on a screen. In the back of the room, Secret Service agents guard a mysterious door.

Tiny, furry animals invade the room and demand that the mysterious door be opened. They threaten to stink up the West Wing with a loaded skunk if their demands are not met. A standoff ensues. A Life Coach named Mindee is called in to mediate. And, through the influence of President
Bush, a tennis club employee, named Roary Goodbuzz, is promoted to Secretary of Environmental Intelligence.

Roary accidentally opens the door and Recyclone escapes. He was being held prisoner by neo conservatives! With hope renewed, Recyclone and his furry friends leave on an extended road trip to convince people to care about the earth once more.

The book never got off my shelf. The election changed things so quickly that I felt the material was out of date.

But here's samples of what the first few pages looked like . . .

The End?

How fitting that the 20th anniversary story ends with me, Lee P. Sauer, carried off stage by right wing thugs and Recyclone flying off for unknown adventures.

Distance came between us in our relationship as well. After the comic strip ended, the feeling was different. Recyclone and I were passing over conquered lands, not discovering new territory. One day, Recyclone gave me that patented smile. Then he turned into a whirlwind and took off. The last I saw of him, he appeared as a speck above a cloud . . . .

Oh, shoot.

I can't do this any more. I'm sorry.

Enough is enough.

I have a confession. For the first time publicly, I admit that I—Lee P. Sauer, one-time mild-mannered reporter for the *Evening Star* newspaper—am The Recyclone.

The stage shows were a sham. That was me in the blue tights and red mask. The Recyclone was simply a product of my imagination.

What about the muscles? Foam padding.

The authoritative voice? Acting.

The vacant expression? I don't know what you're talking about.

I can understand, though, your skepticism. I worked hard to keep the secret.

When playing Recyclone, I did my best to stay in character. If I wore the costume, I walked and talked like Recyclone. And, like my fellow alter ego geeks Bruce Wayne and Clark Kent, when dressed as myself, I denied any superhero connection.

Maintaining a dual identity proved tough. As I walked through schools, students would point at me and say, "You're that recycling man!"

"No, I'm not," I would reply. "I'm just a nerdy cartoonist."

For Recyclone shows, I painted an old refrigerator box to look like a recycling center. Inside the box I made the transition from nerd to superhero, and visa versa. A curtain across the back of the box alone separated me from the wider world.

At the end of a show, Recyclone would duck into the box to change into me. Quite often, while I was pulling on my pants, a few of the more mischievous students, despite a teacher's order to stay in line, ventured back and peaked through the curtain.

"You're that recycling man!"

"No I'm not."

"Then where is he?"

"He ... um ... turned into a cyclone and flew away."

No matter how certain their convictions and smug their expressions, the kids almost always glanced up, just to make sure.

Those kids are now 30 to 40 years old. They have children of their own. And mortgages. They can't be so easily fooled.

But hopefully they have deep within themselves the magic of Recyclone—the idea that anyone, no matter how limited, has the power to save the earth. All it requires is that each person play a small role: care a little, be informed a little, sacrifice a little.

The curtain has been pulled back. There is no superhero. The Recyclone is us.

There's work to be done.

The fate of the earth hangs in the balance.

The Recyclone by Lee P.

Lee P. Sauer lives in Angola, IN, with his three lovely daughters. He makes his living through freelance writing, illustration and handyman work.

Sauer grew up in Indiana and Illinois. He received a degree in Education from Concordia University in Forest Park, IL, in 1980. For four years he taught elementary school—two years each in Torrance, CA, and Fort Wayne, IN.

Hoping to become a writer and cartoonist, Sauer pursued a variety of jobs. He worked as a commercial fisherman in Kodiak, AK; as a newspaper reporter in Wittenberg, WI; as a t-shirt artist in Fort Wayne, IN, and as a reporter in Auburn, IN.

Sauer is the author of several books, including "It's a Duesey!" "The Many Lives of Glenn T. Rieke," and "Drawing From History: Abraham Lincoln."